BATTLING DEMONS

My Story

PAUL CHANDLER

ISBN 979-8-89428-482-8 (paperback)
ISBN 979-8-89428-483-5 (digital)

Christian Faith Publishing
832 Park Avenue
Meadville, PA 16335
www.christianfaithpublishing.com

Printed in the United States of America

INTRODUCTION

I never went to church much before I met my wife. I could count on one hand how many times I went. I started going to church with her occasionally. Then we got married and had a son about eighteen months after. Shortly after our son's birth, I got saved.

We've gone to several different churches through the years. All the churches we've been to, I couldn't recall any sermons that was totally about Satan or demons or even hell. Satan and hell got mentioned in sermons once in a while.

It's like the pastors were afraid of preaching about them because they didn't want to upset anyone or scare them off. Congregations would rather hear about the good side of God's Word. Satan, demons, and hell are all part of God's Word too and needs to be studied in the same manner as the rest of God's Word in the Bible. That's why it's in there. If you're going to claim to be a Christian, you can't ignore this side of his Word. You have to know it all. If you don't study both sides of it, then it's the same as being half a Christian, and there is no such thing; you either are or you're not. God put it in the Bible so you'll know what you're up against and know how to protect yourself and others.

I never knew why I had to experience demons all my life 'till God came to me and asked me to go around to churches and talk about them and write this book to get the word out so people will know how important it is to study the whole Bible, not just half of it. If you notice that in all the words in red that are Jesus's, he talks about and deals with the evil side more than anything else.

This is the first book I've ever written. I never dreamed that I would be an author someday. God can give you the ability to do whatever he asks of you. He has helped me with this all the way.

This might be small as far as books go, but it got some powerful information in it. There's also a lot of education on demons in it. I thank God for giving me a job to do for him after all these years. I'm fifty-nine years old at the writing of this, and God is just now using me. You're never too old to work for God.

CHAPTER 1

My Battle

God has been letting me experience something all my life. I have never known why I had to experience it 'till recently. God came to me and told me he had something he wanted me to do for him, so I said yes.

It started out as going around to churches and giving a talk. I sat down and was going to write down some bullet points to give my talk on, but when I started writing them down, I started to write in book form which I hadn't intended to do. So I thought to myself, *I guess I'm supposed to write a book also.*

I went ahead and wrote what I wanted to talk about to the churches, and then I backed up and started writing it in a book version with a lot more added to it. So here's my story:

God sometimes lets people experience something so they can gain knowledge of it so they can share the experience with others. Sometimes, you experience something that's good, full of joy and Gods love. And sometimes, you'll experience something that is full of evil and will scare your socks off.

I've never told anyone about these experiences until my wife noticed me going through them in my sleep. She probably thought I was just having nightmares instead of knowing what was really going on. I guess I felt that if I told anyone about them, they would think I was crazy.

The things I have been experiencing are not from the joyful side of things but the evil side.

Ephesians 6–12 (NIV) states, For our struggle is not against flesh and blood, but against the rulers, against the authorities, against the powers of this world and against the spiritual forces of evil in the heavenly realm.

The thing I'm talking about is demon encounters. I've always wondered why I have had to go through them so much.

It's because God wanted me to see how real they are and be able to share this with you. So you will have a witness to tell you that demons are out there, and they're very real.

The encounters are not to be confused with demonic possession as it is not the same thing. They use the same methods but for different purposes. With possession, they take over your mind and body and use it to walk the earth for their evil purposes. With encounters, they control your body and mind to torment you. The demons are with you, but they are not totally inside of you.

Billy Graham states that scholars estimate that one-third of the angels cast their lot with Satan when he mysteriously rebelled against his Creator. One's who are now desperate demons, Lucifer and his angels turned into demons.

Demons are going to come after you when you are most vulnerable and least expect it. And when you're asleep is one of those times.

I'm going to talk to you about some of my experiences with them. I'll describe them as best as I can. It would be impossible to explain some of the things they do because they are from an evil realm and have powers that are indescribable, so I won't even try.

When they come to me, they appear as shadow figures. They have no face or features that I can see. They just look like a shadow on the wall. It's hard to tell how many there are because they are continually moving and circling me. They bump into me and shove me, and they all keep getting closer to me. I really don't care how many there are because all I want to do is get away from them. But there is no escape from them because they control my mind and body. They continue getting closer to me until I can't breathe anymore. And because they are controlling my mind, I can't think about what to do to stop them. Because they are controlling my body, I can't even move to try to get away. I am in their realm while this is happening. My body hasn't moved from where I am, but a part of me is with them.

You have two battles going on: one with the demons and one in your mind trying to get it to work again. When these attacks start, you have no knowledge of anything or anyone, including God. You must fight to get your mind back and remember that God is there so you can ask him for help because you can't defeat demons on your own. It's hard winning your mind back while they are tormenting you. After I get my mind back and remember that God is my only hope, I pray a simple prayer that has a lot of power in it to chase them away. It is, Demons, get away from me in the name of Jesus. I don't want you here; you don't belong here. I pray that repeatedly until they leave, which doesn't take long because they know God has control of them. Then I can wake up and breathe again.

Good and evil cannot exist in the same place. I feel that the only way they can come after me is that God must leave me so that they can come in. And then I must fight my way back to God to get rid of them. Below are two verses that back this up:

Now the spirit of the Lord departed from Saul and a harmful spirit from the Lord tortured him. (1 Samuel 16:14)

And the Lord said unto Satan, very well then, everything he has is in your power, but on the man himself do not lay a finger. (Job 1:12 NIV)

The verse from Job shows that God has control over Satan and his demons, and they can only do what God lets them do.

Most of the visits are like the one I just described, but every time one of these happens, it all starts over again. I can't think. I can't move. I don't know God. Even though I have dealt with them before, they are just as scary as the first time.

I can also clearly remember an encounter when I was a little kid. I'm not sure how old I was, maybe five years old.

They approached me the same way as they do now. I couldn't move, but I could think and talk. This time, I think they let me think and talk because I didn't know God at that age. I can remember talking to them, but they didn't talk back. They just kept wandering around me. And one picked me up and was holding me.

I can remember being scared, but I didn't realize what they were either. Since I didn't know what they were, I was talking to them to try to make friends with them so they wouldn't hurt me and leave me alone. At this point, they took my voice away so I couldn't talk anymore. Evidently, they didn't want any new friends.

Since I didn't know God, I didn't know about praying to ask him for help, so they stayed with me until they were done with me.

Now, I ask myself why they would come and torment me when I was a little kid. I think they knew my future and what path was ahead of me. I believe they were trying to alter my path. Why else would one have held me like it did as if to say you're safe here; hang out with us.

I believe I have stayed on the path that God had for me though. And along with my wife, we created a daughter that has a huge heart for God, and along with her husband, they pastor a church. And I believe they also knew that God was going to use me to do this book later in life. And they were trying to stop all this even back then. I can't remember any other visits during my younger childhood. If there were any, I have forgotten them. Maybe God thought this one visit was enough to remember to talk about. I can remember it as if it happened yesterday.

I have also had one visit that woke me up before it started. It was actually an attack this time.

I had worked at an event in Columbus, Ohio, as a paramedic, and after it was over, I went to my regular firehouse to spend the night because it was late, and I had to be there the next morning for my regular shift. I walked in, found me a room, made my bed, took a shower, and lay down to go to sleep.

4

This station has individual rooms instead of the large dorm room like some older stations. You are by yourself in the room.

After I went to sleep, I would say that it was about an hour or so before I woke up, and something didn't feel right. It's like I could sense something out in the hallway: a presence.

Then I could feel the presence start moving toward the door to my room, and then it stopped. Then I felt the presence come through the door. You know how when you're sitting in your house in the evening and the temperature outside is cooling down and you can hear popping and cracking noises from the house cooling off. That's what was happening when it came into my room. I could hear popping noises and could feel the pressure in the room increase.

I had no doubt what it was. It was another demon visit, but this one was different. For one thing, I was awake this time. I couldn't see it, but I could feel that it was there. I could tell that it was just one this time, and it was more powerful than all the other ones combined. It's hard to describe what I was feeling while it was near me.

Then it was on. Just like the other visits, I couldn't move or think. I didn't know God again. It stepped toward my bed and put its hands on me. This has never happened before. It started bouncing me and rolling me around on the bed. And since this demon was more powerful, the battle in my mind was harder to fight. After a while, I started gaining ground in my head, and I was able to pray to God to help me get out of this one.

CHAPTER 2

What You Need to Know
to Battle Demons!

For I am persuaded that neither death, nor life, nor angels, nor principalities, nor powers, nor things present, nor things to come, nor height nor depth, nor any other creature shall be able to separate us from the love of God. Which is in Christ Jesus our Lord. (Romans 8:38–39 KJV)

This verse tells me that even though I experience these demons, they cannot separate me from God. If I let them separate me from God, it is my own fault. It is because I wasn't strong enough in the Lord, and my faith in him was weak.

I've been reading books on hell by Bill Wiese. He was sent to hell by God so he could experience it and be able to tell the world about it so he could describe it and tell everyone how real it is, and he paints a vivid picture of it. His first book is titled *23 Minutes in Hell.* If you haven't read it, you should. The demons that he describes that are in hell are thousands of times crueler than the ones I have dealt with, even the one that physically attacked me.

Demons hate God. The more souls they steal from him, the happier they are. I'm sure God cries over all the souls he loses.

The Bible says not to be ignorant of spiritual things. People need to hear about the evil realm so they know that they need to love God and stay away from the evil. God doesn't want you to go to hell. He wants you to be with him, to worship him, and love him and be loved by him. That's why he's using me as a witness to the demons and what they're like and what they are capable of so you'll know what will happen if you don't follow him.

Some people think that if God is so loving, why would he send anyone to hell. They feel that just because they are a good person, they should get a free pass to heaven. They don't realize that it's not God that's sending them to hell, but they're sending themselves to hell by the choices they have made.

I reiterate with this question: Why does God back off and let evil attack a person? He wants that person to really experience evil just like someone that is going to hell to be punished so they can tell others and be able to convince them of the reality—the evil that they will face if they don't get saved. And if you're already saved, to take inventory of yourself, to make sure that you are living the way he wants you to, and to make sure that you fear God and worship him. If you've never had any encounters of your own, consider yourself lucky. But that doesn't mean that you never will. Evil is creeping more into our world every day, and it's building up strength. Demons are good at what they do. They get a lot of practice. A demon's only job is torment and destruction.

So if you ever do encounter anything like this or worse, make sure you have on your full armor of God, and be ready to use it. You need to have your armor on every day. These encounters can happen at any time without warning.

And remember that where God is, there is love and joy, and where he isn't, evil comes in and takes over. So always keep God in your heart and mind so evil won't have a chance with you. I wouldn't wish my experiences onto anyone.

> And these signs shall follow them that believe;
> in my name shall they cast out devils; they shall
> speak with new tongues. (Mark 16:17 KJV)

Every Christian can cast out demons in the name of Christ. Of course, you have had to kneel and ask for forgiveness of your sins and declare that you believe that Christ died on the cross and rose from the dead on the third day. You must be a biblically clean vessel. Our hearts must be washed continually by obeying His Word. We must confess all known sin and recognize our position as under the blood of Jesus.

If we walk in this way, we need to simply command the evil spirits to come out in Jesus's name. Use authority when you do it. You shouldn't be afraid of the devil and his demons. You should stand and face them and cast them away from yourself and others. God is with you. He'll protect you. You can do it.

> Submit yourselves therefore to God. Resist the
> devil, and he will flee from you. (James 4:7 KJV)

There was a time I was afraid of them but not anymore. I'll stand and face them and resist anything they throw at me.

Even after I was attacked by one, I wasn't afraid. While I was laying there afterward, I just thought, *Wow, that was different.*

Maybe that is why God has let this happen to me so much. The more I dealt with them, the less they could scare me, and I can be a good witness to tell the world that they are real, and I won't let them separate me from God.

You can tell by watching what's going on in the world where demons hang out more than others. They are in control in cities around the world where people believe in other religions. And also where there are more people in general that refuse to follow God. This could be any place such as a neighborhood even.

Some people wonder where the demons go after they are cast out. You can tell them where to go when you cast them out like into the void of space or an uninhabited region on the earth, but the devil will release them from where you sent them, so it doesn't do much good to tell them where to go. Just tell them not to come back to where they were cast out from. And don't bother telling them to go back to hell where they came from because they haven't been there yet. And they will know that you don't know what you are doing and not leave. They can't go to hell until Jesus sends them there at the end of the age, and they will be bound there with the devil forever. For now, they will continue to walk the earth or find someone else to dwell in. Demons never die.

Demons will try to find someone that has an open door to them—people that mess around with witchcraft or voodoo, play with Ouija boards, hang out in places that have evil going on at it even if you're not participating in it, have idols from other religions, people that follow astrology and do what they tell you to do. Some things that seem so innocent can get you in big trouble down the road.

The sheer number of demons on the earth is innumerable. The number of angels in heaven is described as ten thousand times ten thousand and thousands of thousands. When Satan was cast down to earth, about a third of the angels came with him. You wouldn't be able to stay in your right mind or step foot anywhere if you could see how many of them there are around you. That's a lot of demons looking for someone to torment.

> Behold, I give you the power to tread on ser-
> pents and scorpions, and over all the power of
> the enemy, and nothing shall by any means hurt
> you. (Luke 10:19 KJV)

Jesus originally gave power to do these things in his name to the original twelve apostles then to the seventy. And then it was given to us.

We must know our enemy to defeat him. That's why I'm telling you all of this. You need to study on this part of his Word as well as the rest of his Word.

We pray in Jesus's name all the time. If we can pray in his name for other needs, we can also pray in his name to cast out demons. You must be strong in God and strong in your faith when doing this. Your strength and faith can weaken while you are fighting them if you don't concentrate on God. They can sense when you're wavering and know if they can beat you. Remember, God won't let you get hurt. Of course, it's a different situation if you are possessed. Another person must recognize it and cast out the demon for you because he is in complete control of you, and you just can't do it yourself because you don't realize what's happening to you.

CHAPTER 3

Demons at Work

Some of the names for demons in the Bible are spirit of infirmity, dumb and deaf spirit, unclean spirit, blind spirit, an angel, a lying spirit, seducing spirits, jealousy spirit, a foul spirit, and a familiar spirit. A familiar spirit is one that can trick you easily. Anglican evangelist Trevor Dearing says these are evil spirits who are familiar with a dead person's appearance, habits, and life.

They imitate the deceased to lead mourners astray into occultism. Such experiences are both real and supernatural. It is also false. This leads people to mediums and their seances. Mediums are also possessed by the familiar spirit.

> For such are false prophets, deceitful workers, transforming themselves into apostles of Christ. And no marvel; For Satan himself is transforming into an angel of light. Therefore, it is no great thing if his ministers also be transformed as the ministers of righteousness; whose end will be according to their works. (2 Corinthians 11:13–15 KJV)

> When someone tells you to consult a medium or spiritualist, who whispers and mutters: should

not a people inquire of their God? Why consult
the dead on behalf of the living? (Isaiah 8:19
NIV)

There are two "Christian sects" that are taking off and growing
now. One calls themselves Annihilationism. They believe in eternal
life after death but not eternal damnation. They can't see why God
would send anybody to hell forever to be tortured even for a minor
sin. They believe that you'll eventually be annihilated after a time
without being sent to hell. But the Bible clearly states when you go
to hell, it's forever.

And these shall go away into everlasting torment;
but the righteous into life eternal. (Matthew
25:46 KJV)

They just twist the verses about it to suit what they want to
hear. John Wesham (vice principal of Tyndale Hall, Bristol, England)
says it speaks of sadism and not justice, and he doesn't know how to
preach on eternal damnation without negating the glory of God.

The other church that is growing rapidly is Universalism. A
universalist believes that every human that God created will finally
come to enter eternal salvation into which Christians enter here and
now. It is argued that God has a universal salvific intention—that
is, a purpose for saving everybody—and that eventually God must
achieve that purpose.

It is his intent to save everyone but not in this way. I believe that
the pastors in these churches are possessed and guided by demons.

The pastors are telling people that there is basically no hell, not
to worry about it, and creating confusion. That you're okay with God
no matter what you do. The verses in the Bible that they are twisting
clearly state the way it is, and it cannot be changed.

Each demon has only one purpose in their existence: they are
named by what their purpose is. If you have something going wrong
in your life, learn about spiritual warfare just in case there is a spiritual reason behind it.

The devil doesn't come to you in a red cape with horns and a pitchfork; he comes to you as everything you ever wished for. I've read several stories of demonic attacks, and there's no end to how they will torture you, injure you, and mess with your life, anything to distract you from God.

One thing that's interesting is that Jewish people don't believe in demons anymore. Traditionally, they did, but as time has gone on, they believe their numbers have gotten fewer and that if you didn't bother them, they wouldn't bother you. Now most Jews don't believe they exist anymore. I watched a rabbi's video, and he was talking about this.

I believe there is evidence of world leaders and military men being possessed by demons and were under their influence. Some of the world's leaders are responsible for murdering millions of people. Some examples of this are the following:

- Kim Il Sung of North Korea murdered 1.6 million of his own people.
- Cambodian leader Pol Pot murdered 1.7 million people.
- Ismail Pasha of Ottoman Empire murdered 2.5 million people.
- Hideki Tojo of Japan murdered 5.2 million people.
- Belgium King Leopold II murdered eight million of his own people.
- Adolph Hitler of Germany murdered 25 million people of which 6 million were Jews.
- Mao Zedong of China murdered an estimated 50 to 75 million of his own people.

There's no way any of these men weren't possessed by demons, and the list is a lot longer than this. And their militaries have all got to be possessed also to follow the orders that they give.

Also, you have to look at cult leaders that's responsible for the deaths of a lot of people. I have only three for example, but there's a lot more of them. I'll go more in-depth on these as it's something we have to deal with more often.

One of the cults that is well-known is Jonestown. The Jonestown massacre occurred on November 18, 1978. There were more than nine hundred members of a cult called the Peoples Temple that died in a mass suicide murder. It took place in the country of Guyana under the leadership of Jim Jones. The cult started in Indiana in the 1950s then was moved to California in the 1960s. In the 1970s, it started getting negative media attention, so the controlling preacher moved it to the Guyanese jungle where he promised them a utopian society.

On November 18, 1978, US Representative Leo Ryan went to investigate claims of abuse. He and four members of his delegation were killed after they arrived at the airstrip. Later that same day, Jones ordered his followers to ingest poison-laced punch while armed guards stood by. Parents had to give their own children a cyanide-laced drink to kill them first and then line up under armed guard to take it themselves. Jim Jones was found in his chair with a bullet wound to his head, most likely self-inflicted.

The next one is Heaven's Gate. The cult was led by Marshall Applewhite—a music professor who, after surviving a near-death experience in 1972, was recruited into the cult by one of his nurses: Bonnie Lu Nettles. In 1975, they persuaded a group of twenty people from Oregon to abandon their families and move to Eastern Colorado where they were promised that an extraterrestrial spaceship would take them to the "kingdom of heaven." They explained to them that human bodies were merely containers that could be abandoned in favor of a higher physical existence.

As the spaceship never showed up, the cult diminished.

In the early 90s, Applewhite started the cult again. He convinced people that after the comet Hale-Bopp was discovered in 1995, a spaceship was hidden in the tail of the comet. When it passed by earth in 1997, he convinced his followers to drink a mixture of phenobarbital and vodka and then lay down to die hoping to leave their bodily containers, enter the spaceship, and pass through heaven's gate into a higher existence.

The last one I'll talk about is more modern-day and is going on in Kenya, Africa.

Pastor Paul Makenzi who heads the Good News International Church is accused of luring his followers to a ranch near the town of Malindi. He allegedly told them to fast to death in order to meet Jesus before burying them in shallow graves across his land. As of May of 2023, the death total is 201 bodies with another six hundred missing.

CHAPTER 4

Some Thoughts

> Do not believe every spirit but test the spirits to see whether they are from God. Because many false prophets have gone out into the world. This is how you can recognize the spirit of God. Every spirit that acknowledges that Jesus Christ has come into the flesh is from God. But every spirit that does not acknowledge Jesus is not from God. This is the spirit of the antichrist. (1 John4:1–3 NIV)

Some people wonder why God lets the demons roam the earth. I believe he does it because you can't have good without evil. If there wasn't any evil, then there wouldn't be any reason to seek God out. God wouldn't have anyone wanting to go to heaven to be with him because there would be no incentive to it. If there is no evil, there is nothing to fear. No eternal damnation, no reason to find God to rescue you from evil. We would just exist without having a reason to live for, and love wouldn't mean anything.

As I wrap up this this section, I want to leave you some things to think about. The next few paragraphs are from my talk I do at churches. I thought I'd leave them unchanged.

First, God tasked me with talking to you about demons. He let this happen to me almost all my life preparing me for this. He doesn't want any of you to experience this evil for eternity. The Bible states that you need to study this.

> My people are destroyed for lack of knowledge:
> (Hosea 4:6 NIV)

Secondly, some people might think this is the rantings of a crazy man. They'd say you're just having nightmares, or you are possessed and trying to confuse or deceive us. I can assure you they are not nightmares. I've had nightmares, and they don't even compare to demon encounters. When you are fighting demons, you are in their realm.

Thirdly, believe that you do have the power in Christ to chase these demons away. Stay strong in God and your faith. We all must stand up to them together; there's strength in numbers. Don't let them separate you from God.

> He that believeth on me, the works I do, shall he
> do also; and greater works than these shall he do.
> (John 14:12)

Fourthly, be careful where you go and what you do. You could open a door to let them in. And God won't stop them if you invite them in. Even if you do it unintentionally.

I've given you Bible verses to back up everything I've told you. Everything I've said is the truth. I prayed to God for help in getting this information and putting together this talk, and he showed me the way through it all. If I needed more information, he would lead me to it, and there's a lot more I could tell you, but I can't keep you here for days. It still amazes me that he picked me to do the work on this subject for him. A lot of people don't want to hear this or talk about it because it scares them. They rather come to church and just hear about the goodness and love of God. But everyone needs to know about demons too. There are a lot of people that say they're Christians who don't believe in demons. They say that they are just symbols of evil, and they're not real.

Believe me, this is not easy to get out in front of people and talk about. It takes a lot of courage on my part to tell of my experiences because I know some people will ridicule me for telling a giant tale and tell me to take my medication.

Just take everything I've said seriously. I'm doing this because I love you all like Jesus wants me to. It was his biggest commandment before he rose up to heaven: "Love each other like I love you." He doesn't want you to go through anything that I have or suffer in eternal damnation.

CHAPTER 5

Spiritual Warfare

I mentioned earlier about spiritual warfare and the armor of God. In this chapter, I am going to break down what spiritual warfare is and describe the armor of God.

Spiritual warfare is not a battle that you physically fight. It is about being ready if the dark forces should come and torment you and try to drag you away from God.

Ephesians 6:10–18 talks about spiritual warfare:

> Finally, be strong in the Lord and in his mighty power. Put on the full armor of God, so you can take your stand against the Devils schemes. For our struggle is not against flesh and blood, but against the rulers, against the authorities, against the powers of this dark world and against the spiritual forces of evil in the heavenly realms. Therefore, put on the full armor of God, so that when the day of evil comes, you may be able to stand your ground, and after you have done everything, to stand. Stand firm then, with the belt of truth buckled around your waist, with the breastplate of righteousness in place. And with your feet fitted with the readiness that comes

with the gospel of peace. In addition to all this, take up the shield of faith, with which you can extinguish all the flaming arrows of the evil one. Take the helmet of salvation and the sword of the spirit, which is the word of God. And pray in the spirit on all occasions with all kinds of prayers and requests. With this in mind, be alert and always keep on praying for all the Lord's people. (Ephesians 6:10–18 NIV)

Now I am going to expand and explain some of the verses.

Verse 10 states to be strong in the Lord. You cannot fight the dark realm on your own. You need the strength of God in you to help battle the evil ones. Demons have too much power to take them on yourself. They could do anything they wanted to without any resistance unless you have the strength of God in you.

Verse 11 tells you to put on the full armor of God. You need to have your armor on and ready to go at all times. You never know when the evil side is going to come after you, and you'll need to be ready to fight back against it. The armor of God is the protection he gives you to do battle.

Verse 12 talks about who our battle is actually with. Our battle is not against anyone on the earth but in the spiritual realm, against the rulers—the top level of the evil spiritual forces. The authorities are like division leaders. And against the spiritual forces of evil in the heavenly realm, which are the foot soldiers that go around tormenting and destroying people and things on earth.

Verse 13 reiterates putting on the full armor of God so you can stand your ground.

Now we get into the full armor of God and each part and its purpose.

Verse 14 states to stand firm with the belt of truth buckled around your waist. The belt of truth means protecting yourself with the truth of God. The devil is going to tell you lies about God that are believable. Knowing the Scriptures will help you defend yourself against these lies.

The breastplate of righteousness is also in place to protect yourself; the breastplate of righteousness means to claim for yourself the righteousness before God that only comes from Christ and then grow in obedience to Christ with his help. Jesus's death means you no longer need to strive to be justified through your own actions. You simply claim by faith the righteous character of God made available to you through Jesus.

Verse 15 discusses the feet. The shoes you put on are the readiness that comes from the gospel of peace. You must be fully prepared. You have to have your peace with God in order to spread his peace to everyone else.

Verse 16 is about the shield of faith. The shield of faith will help you stop the flaming arrows that the devil will throw at you. Flaming arrows being lies, accusations, or anything that brings your spirit down. You have to keep your faith strong so you can recognize what the devil is doing to you and be able to fight it off. And you need to know God's Word so that you will know when you are being lied to.

Verse 17 talks about the helmet and the sword. You put on the helmet of salvation by believing that Christ died for your sins and rose again. Your salvation should always be at the front of your mind. The sword of the spirit is the Word of God. It is your greatest weapon in the battle of the dark realm. It is the only piece of equipment you have that you can go on the offensive when in spiritual warfare. The rest of the armor is there for defense to protect you.

Verse 18 reminds you to pray. You need to pray without ceasing about everything and to pray for the Lord's people for their protection.

There are two other scriptures that you can also use to be ready for spiritual warfare:

> And do this, understanding the present time; the hour has already come for you to wake up from your slumber, because our salvation is nearer now than when we first believed. The night is nearly over; the day is almost here. So let us put aside the deeds of darkness and put on the armor of

light. Let us behave decently, as in the daytime, not in carousing and drunkenness, not in sexual immorality and debauchery, not in dissension and jealousy. Rather, clothe yourselves with the Lord Jesus Christ, and do not think about how to gratify the desires of the flesh. (Romans 13:11– 14 NIV)

Paul writes of the "armor of light" which is a metaphor about living an honest and honorable life. If you keep things secret about sinful thoughts, it's like living in the dark. When you put on the "armor of light," you must be honest about your temptations and be transparent with trusted friends about where you need God's help. The result is being closer to Christ and being ready for spiritual warfare.

Another verse is 1 Thessalonians 5:8:

But since we belong to the day, let us be sober, putting on faith and love as a breastplate, and the hope of salvation as a helmet. (1 Thessalonians 5:8 NIV)

The passage in both Romans and Thessalonians talks about the day. This is a reference when Jesus will return to the earth. The passage in Romans also says the night is nearly over. That means the evil realm is running out of time 'till Jesus returns.

Remember that through all of this spiritual warfare, God is with you. He will protect you and give you everything you need to do battle.

You have probably heard the phrase "spiritual warfare" around Christians a lot. But even though they say it, not all really understand what it is. Spiritual warfare is not actually a physical battle as we see between people here on earth. Spiritual warfare involves a strong prayer life and making yourself strong in God so that the devil doesn't even want to waste his time on you. Because he knows he won't get anywhere. You have to know the scriptures that deal with spiritual warfare so that if he does try to come at you with his lies to draw you away from God, you can use the sword of the spirit to fight back at him.

The devil will tell you things that you think you want to hear such as being in control of yourself instead of letting God be in control. Most people want to resist giving over control to God because they think they're strong enough to handle things on their own. The devil knows this and will use this weakness to control you.

The devil knows you better than what you think. He studies you to find out all your weaknesses so he can use them against you. He probably knows you better than you know yourself.

Another part of spiritual warfare is helping others to get stronger in God and pray for them and pray for the unsaved. The more people that are saved and strong in God, the less people the devil will have to pick from to keep from God.

And just like the devil studies you, you need to study about him and his demons. You need to know your enemy if you are going to fight against him.

Paul writes in Romans 7:21–23 (NIV),

> So I find this law at work: Although I want to do good, evil is right there with me. For in my inner being I delight in God's law; But I see another law at work in me. Waging war against the law of my mind and making me a prisoner of the law of sin at work within me.

This describes that no matter how strong you are in your mind with God, the flesh is still right there with you. The flesh fights you from within, hindering everything that you know you need to do.

When Jesus died on the cross, the devil was defeated at that point. When he was resurrected, it showed that he had victory over death. This is where the devil comes in with his lies to confuse people as to what Jesus had actually done.

He comes to you in many ways to deceive you. Coming to you as an ally is one of his easiest ways of drawing you away from God. He plants thoughts in your head to cast doubts on what you know.

He bends what God is telling you to make it seem like God is working against you, not for you. That's why it is important to have the armor of God on to help protect you.

The devil is real and dangerous. Be careful how you do battle with him. Don't go against him alone. God has placed the Holy Spirit in you to help you do battle with him.

The following verses can be used to prepare yourself when you are battling the world, the flesh, or the devil:

> For though we live in the world, we do not wage war as the world does. The weapons we fight with are not the weapons of the world. On the contrary, they have divine power to demolish strongholds. We demolish arguments and every pretention that sets itself up against the knowledge of God, and we take captive every thought to make it obedient to Christ. (2 Corinthians 10:3–5 NIV)

> No weapon forged against you will prevail, and you will refute every tongue that accuses you. This is the heritage of the servants of the Lord, and this is their vindication from me, declares the lord. (Isaiah 54:17 NIV)

CHAPTER 6

Demons Throughout the Bible

This chapter is going to be dealing with demons throughout the Bible. Demons are in the Bible from start to finish. All demons have a purpose. It can be anything from making you chronically ill to doing anything it can to mess up your life to distract you from seeking God. The names the demons have in the Bible were given to them due to the type of things they do to torment people and things that were going on in that period and the lifestyles of the people back then also.

But now, things are totally different, there's a lot more things that didn't exist back then that demons can use against you in your life that aren't named in the Bible.

I'm going to go through these by groups of the different types but not in the order they are in the Bible.

The first one I'll do is the spirit of infirmity. An infirm spirit is mentioned once in the Bible. Jesus healed many people with infirmities, but not all of them are caused by spirits.

> And a woman was there who had been crippled by a spirit for eighteen years. She was bent over and could not straighten up at all. When Jesus saw her, he called her forward and said to her, "woman, you are set free from your infirmity."

> Then he put his hands on her, and immediately
> she straightened up and praised God. (Luke
> 13:11–13 NIV)

This verse shows you how long a demon can torment you without anyone knowing that it is the cause behind whatever your problem may be. People that can't recognize that it's a demon just think that it's a health problem that can't be cured. But then Jesus came along and cast the demon out, and she was cured.

A spirit of infirmity can use anything health-wise against you. It doesn't have to be anything as bad as what they did to this woman. It could be constant headaches, something wrong with an organ in your body, or something paralyzing among others. If you look around, you can see how much infirmity is in the world. It's running rampant with diseases and afflictions everywhere. Spirits of infirmity are busy. Most of the world doesn't consider that it could be demons causing the majority of it. Doctors treat the illness with medicine unsuccessfully when it's demons that need casting out. But that doesn't mean that all infirmities are caused by demons.

The next one is the dumb and deaf spirit. This spirit takes away the ability to hear and speak, not allowing you to communicate with other people.

The story that is an example of this spirit happens right after Jesus's transfiguration.

> When they came to the other disciples, they saw
> a large crowd around them and the teachers of
> the law arguing with them. As soon as all the
> people saw Jesus, they were overwhelmed with
> wonder and ran to greet him.
> "What are you arguing with them about?"
> Jesus asked.
> A man in the crowd answered, "Teacher, I
> brought you my son, who is possessed by a spirit
> that has robbed him of his speech. Whenever
> it seizes him, it throws him to the ground.

He foams at the mouth, gnashes his teeth and becomes rigid. I asked your disciples to drive out the spirit, but they could not."

"You unbelieving generation," Jesus replied, "how long shall I stay with you? How long shall I put up with you? Bring the boy to me."

So they brought him. When the spirit saw Jesus, it immediately threw the boy into a convulsion. He fell to the ground and rolled around, foaming at the mouth.

Jesus asked the boy's father, "How long has he been like this?" "From childhood," he answered.

"It has often thrown him into fire or water to kill him. But if you can do anything, take pity on us and help us.

"'If you can'?" said Jesus. "Everything is possible for one who believes."

Immediately the boy's father exclaimed, "I do believe; help me overcome my unbelief!"

When Jesus saw that a crowd was running to the scene, he rebuked the impure spirit. "You deaf and mute spirit," he said, "I command you, come out of him and never enter him again."

The spirit shrieked, convulsed him violently and came out. The boy looked so much like a corpse that many said, "He's dead." But Jesus took him by the hand and lifted him to his feet, and he stood up.

After Jesus had gone indoors, his disciples asked him privately, "Why couldn't we drive it out?"

He replied, "This kind can come out only by prayer." (Mark 9:14–29 NIV)

In this story, Jesus is teaching about the power of faith and prayer. The father here is only human, and his faith is weakening. He wants to trust Jesus, but his fear is overcoming him. He asks Jesus to help him with his faith. Jesus also chastises his disciples for their weak faith. If their faith was stronger, they could have cast it out. This shows that they are only human also. This story shows that some demons are harder to cast out than others.

Next, I'll cover the impure or unclean spirit; the name impure spirit comes up once in the Old Testament in Zechariah and Matthew, Mark, and Luke in the New Testament.

"On that day a fountain will be opened to the house of David and the inhabitants of Jerusalem, to cleanse them from sin and impurity. On that day, I will banish the names of idols from the land, and they will be remembered no more," declares the Lord Almighty. "I will remove both the prophets and the spirit of impurity from the land."

And if anyone still prophesy, their father and mother, to whom they were born, will say to them, "You must die, because you have told lies in the Lord's name." Then their own parents will stab the one who prophesies.

On that day every prophet will be ashamed of their prophetic vision. They will not put on a prophet's garment or hair in order to deceive. Each will say, "I am not a prophet, I am a farmer; the land has been my livelihood since my youth." If someone asks, "What are the wounds on your body?" They will answer, "The wounds I was given at the house of my friends." (Zechariah 13:1–6 NIV)

Zechariah 13:1–6 is prophesying the day that Jesus was hung and killed on the cross. He died on the cross for our sins so that we would continue to have life. The fountain is Christ. The fountain came out of his side where he was pierced. The fountain flows the blood of Jesus, not water. His blood is what cleanses us from our sins. The fountain is forever flowing.

God is going to banish all the idols so no one will have false gods to follow. The God of Abraham is the only God we should follow. He is getting rid of the false prophets so there will be no more lies told to confuse us and draw us away from God. God is putting it on to the false prophets' parents to kill them if they continue to tell lies in their prophesies. The prophets will be so ashamed that they won't put on their garments and lie about what they really are.

Now we go to the New Testament where Matthew, Mark, and Luke write about the impure spirits.

> When an impure spirit comes out of a person, it goes through arid places seeking rest and does not find it. Then it says, "I will return to the house I left," when it arrives, it finds the house unoccupied, swept clean and put in order.
>
> Then it goes and takes with it seven other spirits more wicked than itself, and they go in and live there. And the final condition of that person is worse than the first. That is how it will be with this wicked generation. (Matthew 12:4–45 NIV)

This story starts by Jesus talking about what happens to a demon when it is cast out. It says they go to arid places; this means that they are cast to where no one else is that they can possess. A demon can only rest when it finds someone else to occupy. It gets tired of wandering around and not being able to do its job.

After a while of running around looking for someone else to occupy, it goes back to the house it was cast out from. In this case, house is another word for a person. It finds the house unoccupied and in order which means it can occupy it again. The man he was cast out of didn't let the Holy Spirit come in to him, so the demon was able to go back into him. If you are cleansed of a demon, you have to let the Holy Spirit in so you will have God's protection covering you.

When the demon sees he can get back in, he goes and gets seven other demons to go with him into the man. These demons are more wicked than the original one. That way, he will have a stronger hold on the man this time and will be harder to cast out again, and the man will be in worse condition this time.

Jesus says that this generation will never stay clean from evil because they won't repent and let the Holy Spirit in, giving evil a stronger foothold.

> They went to Capernaum, and when the Sabbath came, Jesus went into the synagogue and began to teach. The people were amazed at his teaching, because he taught them as one who had authority, not as teachers of the law.
>
> Just then a man in their synagogue who was possessed by an impure spirit cried out, "What do you want with us, Jesus of Nazareth? Have you come to destroy us? I know who you are, the Holy One of God!"
>
> "Be quiet!" said Jesus sternly. "Come out of him!" The impure spirit shook the man violently and came out of him with a shriek.
>
> The people were all so amazed that they asked each other, "What is this? A new teaching, and with authority! He even gives orders to impure spirits and they obey him." News about him spread quickly over the whole region of Galilee. (Mark 1:21–28 NIV)

When the man came up to Jesus and asked him, "What do you want with us?" this clearly shows that it is the impure spirit that is talking and not the man. If it was an unpossessed man, he would of answered in the singular and not the plural. The demon has complete control of the man. The demon also acknowledges that he knows that it is Jesus standing in front of him.

Jesus doesn't take the time to argue with him and immediately tells it to be quiet and come out of the man showing his authority over the demon. The demon gets mad and violently leaves the man because he knows Jesus' power over him, and he can't do anything about it.

It amazes all the people around them that Jesus has the ability and the power to do this and the word about him spread quickly around Galilee.

> They went across the lake to the regions of the Gerasene's. When Jesus got out of the boat, a man with an impure spirit came from the tombs, and no one could bind him anymore. Not even with a chain. For he had often been chained hand and foot, but he tore the chains apart and broke the irons on his feet. No one was strong enough to subdue him. Night and day among the tombs and in the hills he would cry out and cut himself with stones.
>
> When he saw Jesus from a distance he ran and fell on his knees in front of him. He shouted at the top of his voice, "What do you want with me, Jesus, son of the Most High God? In God's name don't torture me." For Jesus had said to him, "Come out of this man, you impure spirit."
>
> Then Jesus asked him, "What is your name?" "My name is Legion," he replied, "for we are many." And he begs Jesus again and again not to send them out of the area.
>
> A large herd of pigs was feeding on the nearby hillside. The demons begged Jesus, "Send us among the pigs; allow us to go into them." He gave them permission and the impure spirits came out and went into the pigs. The herd, about

two thousand in number rushed down the steep
bank into the lake and were drowned. (Mark
5:1–13 NIV)

This story tells of a man with super strength, and he was out of
his mind. He was controlled by an impure spirit. He could not fight
against them because they were so in control of him that he didn't
know who he was. There was nothing anyone could do to help him,
and binding him would not work. All he could do was whatever the
demons would have him do.

He saw Jesus and ran up to him. These demons knew who Jesus
was upon sight and asked him what he wanted with him. He had
respect for Jesus because he knew who he was and what he could do.
The demon also showed respect for God by acknowledging the fact
that he is the Most High God. Demons don't like God, but they still
show respect for him because they are still his creation even though
they fell away from him.

Jesus knew that there was a multitude of demons in him. They
asked Jesus to send them into the pigs because they thought they
would be able to exist in them instead of being cast out into noth-
ingness. Demons were not allowed to occupy animals; this is why
they had to ask permission to go into the pigs. This shows that they
weren't very smart about it because the pigs went crazy and killed
themselves by running over a cliff into the lake. The demons were
left wandering anyway.

Jesus left that place and went into the vicinity
of Tyre. He entered into a house and did not
want anyone to know it; yet he could not keep
his presence secret. In fact, as soon as she heard
about him, a woman whose little daughter was
possessed by an impure spirit came and fell at his
feet. The woman was a Greek. Born in Syrian
Phoenicia. She begged Jesus to drive the demon
out of her daughter.

"First let the children eat all they want," he told her, "For it is not right to take the children's bread and toss it to the dogs." "Lord," she replied, "even the dogs under the table eat the children's crumbs."

Then he told her, "For such a reply, you may go; the demon has left your daughter." She went home and found her child lying on the bed, and the demon gone. (Mark 7:24–30 NIV)

This is a short story, but it says a lot. In it, the children are not actually kids; they are the descendants of Abraham which makes them Israel. The dogs represent the Gentiles. The term Gentile means anyone that is not Jewish. The bread represents the miraculous cure.

The woman is desperate for help healing her daughter. She runs up to Jesus and begs him for his help, showing that even though she is a Gentile, she has great faith in him. But since she is Gentile and not Jewish, he basically tells her to go away. But she persists and won't give up. She has a glimmer of hope since he said first the children must eat, then the dogs will be fed after that. She didn't want to alter Jesus's plans with the Jews being taken care of first. She says a crumb of his help is all she wants. She continues begging him. He must have been impressed with her persistence and her strong faith because, in the end, he helps her daughter.

Now I'll talk about the deceiving spirits. First Kings 22 and 2 Chronicles 18 both talk about a deceiving spirit. They both talk about the same one. I'll use 1 Kings (NIV) for telling about this one. This is the story of Micaiah the prophet and Ahab the king of Israel. I'll use verses 19–25.

Micaiah continued, "Therefore hear the word of the Lord: I saw the Lord sitting on his throne with all the multitudes of heaven standing around him on his right and on his left. And the Lord said, who will entice Ahab into attacking Ramoth Gilead and going to his death there?"

"One suggested this, and another suggested that. Finally, a spirit came forward and stood before the Lord and said, 'I will entice him.' "'By what means?' the Lord asked.

"'I will go out and be a deceiving spirit in the mouths of all his prophets,' he said. "'You will succeed in enticing him,' said the Lord. "Go and do it.'

"So now the Lord has put a deceiving spirit in the mouths of all these prophets of yours. The Lord has decreed disaster for you."

Then Zedekiah son of Kenaanah went up and slapped Micaiah in the face. "Which way did the spirit from the Lord go when he went from me to speak to you?" he asked. Micaiah replied, "You will find out on the day you go hide in an inner room." (1 Kings 22:19–25)

This story shows how the Lord uses impure spirits to do his work also. The spirits are God's creation, and they have to obey him even though they don't like him. In this story, Ahab wants to know what he should do about the city of Ramoth, Gilead. The king of Aram is in control of it, but it belongs to Israel. He first tries to get Jehoshaphat, king of Judah, to go with him and help him. Jehoshaphat says everything he has is for his using. But he won't go until Ahab seeks council of the Lord. So that's when Ahab brought together the prophets, about four hundred men, and asked them, "Shall I go to war against Ramoth, Gilead, or shall I refrain?" They all said go, for the Lord will give it unto the king's hand.

But Jehoshaphat asked, "Is there no longer a Prophet of the Lord here whom we can inquire of." Ahab answered Jehoshaphat, "There is still one prophet whom we can inquire of the lord. But I hate him because he never prophesies anything good about me." In other words, he never tells the king what he wants to hear. He wants everything about him to be good, not bad.

He has Micaiah brought to him to ask him what he should do, and Micaiah tells him like the others that he should go to war and be victorious. Of course, this isn't what he wants to hear because he doesn't want to go to war.

Micaiah went on to tell him about the Lord sitting on his throne. The Lord wants to know who will entice Ahab to go to war. No one had any good ideas, and then a spirit came up to the Lord and said that he would entice him, and the Lord told him to go do it, and he would succeed. Demons are capable of being deceiving more so than humans. They are good at being bad.

> The spirit clearly says that in later times some will abandon the faith and follow deceiving spirits and things taught by demons. Such teachings come through hypocritical liars. Whose consciences have been seared as a hot iron. They forbid people to marry and order them to abstain from certain foods, which God created to be received with thanksgiving, by those who believe and know the truth. For everything God created is good, and nothing is to be rejected if it is received with thanksgiving, because it is consecrated by the word of God and prayer. (1 Timothy 4:1–5 NIV)

When you read these verses and look around yourself at what is going on in today's society, you can see that the deceiving spirits and demons' teachings are in full force.

People are abandoning the faith and following false religions and joining cults. The things that kids in school and adults in college are being taught things that have nothing to do with education but indoctrination into anything that is immoral or evil; they don't know any better because of their upbringing by previous generations that have abandoned God and haven't been given any guidance or teaching about morals and God.

They teach that it's okay to do whatever you want, that nothing is wrong. Just be yourself; it's your life. They are teaching things that are lies and causing division between everyone.

There are always groups telling that certain foods are bad for you and not to eat them. People have been eating these foods for thousands of years since they were created by God with no problem. They want you to eat food that's made in labs instead of what's grown naturally. The latest thing is lab-grown meat. Who knows what they put in this stuff.

People don't care if they get married anymore and just live together and have kids out of wedlock. If they do get married, they don't work at keeping their relationship healthy. They don't live for God anymore; he's an afterthought way down on the list of what's important.

If a problem comes up that causes strife in their marriage, they don't work at it to solve the problem. They just go and get a divorce and then look for another person to live with and maybe marry.

The kids in these bad relationships suffer also because they don't have a stable family; they have to bounce back and forth between two households. They don't really have a homelife, and that messes with their mental health. The parents use the kids to get at each other and make the other parent mad.

Like the verses say, everything God created is good. This includes relationships. God said we are to marry, be fruitful, and multiply, not live together 'till one gets tired of it and leaves. You're in it 'till death do you part. And raise your children to know and love God.

Nowadays, everything that God has created is being downplayed, and people are led to believe that his creation doesn't mean anything anymore.

Now, I'll move on to familiar spirits. These are mentioned throughout the Old Testament. I mentioned this type of spirit in a prior chapter.

A familiar spirit can trick you easily. They imitate the deceased to lead mourners astray into occultism. Such experiences are both real and supernatural; it is also false. This leads people to mediums and spiritists and their seances. Mediums are also possessed by the familiar spirit.

Most of the writing about familiar spirits is about how God wants you to stay away from mediums and spiritists and what his punishment for going to them is. Mediums and spiritists are not of God. They are influenced by demons to draw you away from God.

The first mention of familiar spirits is in Leviticus 19:31 (NIV). This section of Leviticus is when God is giving his laws to Moses to give to the people so they'll know how God wants them to live for him.

> Regard not them that have familiar spirits, nei-
> ther seek after wizards, to be defiled by them: I
> am the LORD your God. (Leviticus 19:31)

The next writing is Leviticus 20:6 (KJV):

> And the soul that turneth after such as have
> familiar spirits, and after wizards, to go a whor-
> ing after them, I will even set my face against that
> soul, and will cut him off from his people.

This verse is in the section that involves the idol Molech. The Lord spoke to Moses and wanted him to tell the children of Israel, or the strangers that travel into Israel, that anyone who sacrifices their children to Molech shall be put to death. The people of the land shall stone them to death.

And God will set his face against that man and cut him off from his people because he sacrificed his child to Molech. It defiles God's sanctuary and profanes God's holy name.

If the people of Israel hide their eyes when a man sacrifices his child to Molech and don't kill him, God will set his face against him and his family and will cut him off from his people and all that go a whoring after him, to commit whoredom with Molech.

A man also or woman that hath a familiar spirit,
or that is a wizard, shall surely be put to death:
They shall stone them with stones: their blood
shall be upon them. (Leviticus 20:27 KJV)

This verse is listed as one of God's laws on what you are to do
when you come across someone that is possessed by a familiar spirit.
The next mention of familiar spirits is in 1 Samuel 28:3:

Now Samuel was dead, and all Israel had lamented
him. And buried him in Ramath, even in his own
city. And Saul had put away those that had familiar spirits, and the wizards, out of the land.

This verse is the story about Saul coming to see Samuel, but
upon arriving, he found out that he had died. He was coming to him
to have him prophesy for him. He was wanting to know what to do
about the Philistines.

Since Samuel was dead, Saul didn't know what to do since it
was his order that had all the people with familiar spirits cast out of
the land.

Then said Saul to his servants, seek me a woman
that has a familiar spirit, that I may go to her, and
inquire of her. And his servants said unto him,
behold, there is a woman that has a familiar spirit
at Endor.

And Saul disguised himself, and put on
other raiment, and he went, and two men with
him, and they came to the woman at night: And
he said: I pray thee, divine unto me by the familiar spirits and bring me him up, whom I shall
name unto thee.

And the woman said unto him, behold,
thou knowest what Saul had done, how he hath
cut off those that have familiar spirits, and the

wizards out of the land: wherefore then layest thou a snare for my life, to cause me to die. (1 Samuel 28:7–9 KJV)

This story tells how Saul is breaking his own law. He is wanting a woman with a familiar spirit to call Samuel up out of Shoel so he can prophesy for him again. Shoel is a place where all the dead go to wait for the Lord to call them up to heaven when it's time. There are two sides to Shoel: one for the wicked that didn't follow God and live for him and the other is for the people that did follow God and live for him.

Saul had disguised himself and went after dark so that no one could see him and that he was breaking his own law. When the woman saw Samuel come up, she knew that it was Saul in disguise and that he deceived her. She was afraid that he had set her up so that he could kill her. But he told her not to worry; he wouldn't do that.

Little did they know that it wasn't Samuel that came up, but it was a familiar spirit that was imitating Samuel. A person with a familiar spirit cannot call anyone up but a familiar spirit.

Now we'll move to 1 Chronicles 10:11–14 (NIV):

When all the inhabitants of Jabesh Gilead heard what the Philistines had done to Saul, all their valiant men went and took the bodies of Saul and his sons and brought them to Jabesh. Then they buried their bones under the great oak tree in Jabesh. And they fasted for seven days.

Saul died because he was unfaithful to the Lord; He did not even keep the word of the Lord and even consulted a medium for guidance, and did not inquire of the Lord. So the Lord put him to death and turned the Kingdom over to David, son of Jessie.

This chapter talks about the Philistines fighting against Israel and also chasing after Saul and his sons. They caught his sons and killed them. The fighting got worse around Saul, and an archer shot him and injured him.

Saul wanted his armor-bearer to kill him so he wouldn't be tormented. His bearer couldn't bring himself to do it, so Saul killed himself.

The Philistines came back the next day and stripped him of his armor and cut off his head. They put his armor in the temple of their gods and his head in the temple of Dagon. Dagon is the father of Baal who is the supreme god of Canaan and Phoenicia.

Saul was going to die one way or another because God wanted him put to death because he was unfaithful and even consulted a medium instead of him.

> In both courts of the temple of the Lord, He built altars to all the starry hosts. He sacrificed his children in the fire in the valley of Ben Hinnom, practiced divination and witchcraft, sought omens, and consulted mediums and spiritists. He did much evil in the eyes of the Lord, arousing his anger. (2 Chronicles 33:5–6 NIV)

This chapter talks about Manasseh becoming king of Judah when he was twelve years old. He reigned for fifty years.

Manasseh did everything evil in the eyes of the Lord that he could think of. He followed all the practices that the Lord had driven out before the Israelites.

He rebuilt the high place that his father Hezekiah had destroyed, erected altars to the Baals, and made Asherah poles. Asherah poles are a sacred tree or pole that stood near the Canaanite religious locations to honor the Ugartic mother-goddess Asherah, consort of El.

He worshipped all the starry hosts. The starry hosts are the sun, moon, and stars. This is astrology, which is a sin. He built altars to the starry hosts in the temple of the Lord.

He also did the things in the verses I started this section with. He led Judah and the people of Jerusalem astray; they did more evil than the nations the Lord had destroyed before the Israelites arrived.

Next, I'll go to Isaiah.

> When someone tells you to consult mediums and spiritists, who whisper and mutter, should not a people inquire of their God? Why consult the dead on behalf of the living? (Isaiah 8:19 NIV)

This part of Isaiah talks about what will happen to people that seek advice from mediums instead of God. Verse 19 talks about mediums and spiritists that whisper and mutter. This means they talk with a low voice, speaking inwardly in their bellies, and not outwardly and audibly with their mouths.

Why would anyone want to consult a medium instead of God? God is the truth and the way while mediums are governed by the father of lies. If people listen to the mediums and spiritists, they will experience suffering. They will be hungry. They will roam through the land. And when they are starved, they will curse their king and their god. They will only see darkness and gloom.

Next, I will go to Deuteronomy 18:

> When you enter the land that the Lord God gives you, do not learn to imitate the detestable ways of the nations there. Let no one be found among you who sacrifices their son or daughter in the fire, who practices divination or sorcery, interprets omens, engages in witchcraft, or casts spells, or who is a medium or spiritist, or who consults the dead. (Deuteronomy 18:9–11 NIV)

These verses are in the section of Deuteronomy where God is giving the law to Moses to give to the people. He is telling the people not to do the detestable things that he is getting rid of ahead of them occupying Israel. They need to be blameless before the Lord.

Second Kings verse 6 is another telling of Manasseh, king of Judah, that I discussed in Isaiah 19.

As you can see by reading these stories that God is strict in his dealings with anyone that is possessed by a familiar spirit or consults with anyone that has a familiar spirit. Like I said at the beginning of this chapter, this is one way that demons can easily deceive you and lure you away from God.

CHAPTER 7

Recognizing Demons

Now, we'll talk a little about recognizing demons.

Demons have been tormenting people for thousands of years. They know what they are doing, and they know how to be not recognized easily. Even the ones that are possessing people are hard to recognize. People that are possessed can be confused with people that have mental issues. These people go to doctors for help, and nothing will work to help them. Medicine will not affect a demon in any way to remove it.

Doctors cannot tell if a demon is in a person just by examining them, especially since they are not looking for them. That is where the demons can affect a person by making them exhibit symptoms that mimics a person having mental issues.

It takes someone with experience with demons to recognize that someone is possessed, and even then, it can be almost impossible to tell if that is what they are dealing with.

The sign that someone is possessed can be subtle. The demon might accidentally reveal itself by doing something that the particular person would not do. Some examples of this might be by exhibiting superhuman strength, letting its real voice come through accidentally, say things that are totally out of character for a person, and terrible attitudes.

Saying something to the person that is experienced in demons that is against God and telling that person to leave "us" alone and to go away. They tend to lose control if you are confronting them with Jesus. They know that once they have been found out and you start to cast them out, there is nothing they can do about it.

Some demons don't care if you know they are possessing a person. These are the more powerful ones to cast out. They can inflict injury to someone or cause them to inflict injury to themselves and hurt other people.

I've read several stories that Lester Sumrall has been involved with.

For example, one is about a girl in South America that people thought had really bad mental issues, and they kept her locked up in a prison cell because they couldn't control her or help her. She had bite marks all over her, and they thought she was doing that to herself. They would find new bite marks on her every day. Lester was down there evangelizing, and the prison officials went to talk to him about her because they were at the end of their rope in dealing with her.

He went to see her and observed all the injuries on her and that some were in places that she couldn't physically reach with her mouth. She was acting quiet and normal at first, and then she started acting up again, screaming and thrashing around. New bite marks were starting to appear on her right in front of everybody, and the new bite marks even had saliva on them as if her or someone else had just freshly bit her, but they could see that no one else around her was doing it.

When he approached her, he found that there were two demons inside her that revealed themselves. He didn't do anything at that time. He went back to his hotel room and prayed and fasted about it for a day.

He went back to her cell to start working on cleansing her of these demons. He told everyone else to move back so that they could see that it was the power of God that was going to cast them out. He didn't want anyone to claim that they did it and try to take God's glory away from him for doing it.

He cast them out, and then they would come back later and would take control of her again. They were so powerful that it took several days of casting them out before they finally stayed away.

There are probably hundreds of ways that they can make you hurt yourself or affect you without anyone realizing that it's a possession and not a medical problem.

The hardest ones to recognize are the demons that attach themselves to you without possessing you. They can affect you without it being a medical issue or make it like you are just having a bad day.

They can make you feel oppressed or depressed, and no one thinks any more about it. This can happen when you're at home, church, or just about anywhere and anytime.

Demons go to church too, so don't think that you're safe because that's where you are. The feeling of oppression is one tactic they use most commonly.

You can be feeling at the top of your game on church day, and when you get there, everything just turns around. You don't realize it's happening to you either, but other people can notice it if they are paying attention to how you changed after you walked in. For example, you're feeling great as you walk up to the church, telling everyone good morning, shaking hands, laughing, and talking. Then when you walk in, you turn into an introvert.

You quit talking, shaking hands, you find a seat and sit there with your head down and don't pay attention to what's going on around you and don't pay attention to the sermon. You don't worship God.

Then when church is over and you leave, you walk out the doors, and the demon releases its grip on you, and you start acting like you did before you went into the church, and you don't realize that it even happened to you.

Another way you can tell if someone has a demon attached to them in church is that the whole time they are sitting there through the service, they will fidget and squirm like they are not comfortable being there.

It's because the demon that attached itself to them doesn't want you to be there. It doesn't want you to be worshipping God. It wants you to get up and leave.

The demons can also cause a person or a child to be a distraction during the service so you can't pay attention to what God wants you to get out of the sermon.

If you'll notice that in most services, children are a distraction because they are crying or talking real loud. The demons will even use the kids because people don't realize that they will go to that extreme.

Don't let the demons win by taking your child out of the service though. Demons will go to any length to distract you from God.

They can also use something outside the church to distract you. Such as a neighbor of the church building. They could be playing loud music, revving noisy cars, mowing the grass with a loud mower. All these can be a distraction from the service.

Demons will also work against you to keep you from going to church to start with.

Things like keeping you up all night so you will be too tired to want to go, causing something to go wrong at home so you will have to stay there and take care of the problem they created.

I've heard a lot of testimonies from people stating that when they get out of bed to go to church, they feel miserable or depressed and thought about staying home. They decide to go to church anyway, and after they get there, they feel much better. That's because they didn't let the demons win by staying home, and God blesses them for it.

Demons are so good at their job that it's really hard to tell if its them that are messing with you.

It's unbelievable how many people that say they are a Christian don't believe in demons or Satan. That they are just "symbols of evil." If you don't believe that they are real, you are basically opening the door and letting them in and not realizing it.

That's why you must study this side of God's Word also. They are real, and they are active.

CONCLUSION

Well, I've come to the end of my first book. It's not very big, but there is a lot of information in it. I believe I got in it everything God wanted me to. I'm not an experienced writer, but I've done my best.

I hope that everyone that reads it gets something out of it and learns a few things, especially where their relationship with God is and that they need to be saved. God's mission for me was to tell my experiences and try to convince people that are unsure of or don't believe in demons that they are very real.

This is not as good as talking to me face-to-face about them, but reading about them can be just as effective, especially if God is with you when you read it.

As I have written this, I could feel the demons fighting against me because they don't want the word out about them and how to get rid of them.

They know their time is running out on this earth, and they are more prevalent tormenting and possessing every day. The end of the age is almost here. That is when they will be sent down into hell with Satan and be imprisoned there with Satan until they are cast into the pit of fire.

Everyone needs to use spiritual warfare every day and get more people to realize they need God to save them. The more people that are saved means the harder it is for the demons to steal souls away from God because it will be harder for them to find someone to attach themselves to.

Pray for each other; love one another like Jesus commanded before he ascended to heaven. I'll be praying for you all that you stay strong in your faith so you'll be able to resist Satan and his minions.

As hard as it will be, don't let evil win. Keep your armor of God on all the time, and be always ready. We are all in this together.

God bless you!

ABOUT THE AUTHOR

Paul lives in the hills of Southeastern Ohio. He has a wife, Leeann, two children, a son, Benjamin, and daughter, Christina, and one grandson named Kieran. He has been a firefighter/paramedic for the past twenty-five years and is encroaching on retirement. Also, he is a cattle farmer.

He and his wife enjoy camping in their RV and plan to spend retirement seeing the country.

Printed in the USA
CPSIA information can be obtained
at www.ICGtesting.com
LVHW091204081024
793244LV00002B/401